p 8 — 1993

Living in Famous Cities

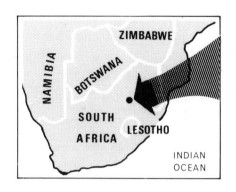

Living in

JOHANNESBURG

Richard Gibbs

Living in Famous Cities

Living in Berlin
Living in Cairo
Living in Calcutta
Living in Hong Kong
Living in Jerusalem
Living in Johannesburg
Living in Madrid
Living in Moscow
Living in New York
Living in Paris
Living in Peking
Living in Rio de Janeiro
Living in Rome
Living in Tokyo

Front cover: View of Johannesburg from one of its gold mines.

Frontispiece: Johannesburg skyscrapers.

82-3063

First published in 1981 by
Wayland Publishers Ltd
49 Lansdowne Place, Hove
East Sussex BN3 1HF, England

© Copyright 1981 Wayland Publishers Ltd

ISBN 0 85340 843 2

Phototypeset by Trident Graphics Ltd,
Reigate, Surrey
Printed and bound in Italy by
G. Canale & C.S.p.A., Turin.

Contents

eGoli – the city of gold   4

From mining camp to modern metropolis   6

The racial problem   8

Living with apartheid   10

The heart of commerce and industry   12

The gold miners   16

The African townships   18

The Coloured, Indian and Chinese quarters   20

The white suburbs   22

Off to school   25

Finding a job   26

On the streets   28

Family life   30

What people eat   32

A day in the park   34

Music and dancing   37

A wealth of religions   38

The thrill of sport   40

Getting around   42

Press, television and radio   44

Urban protest   46

Hillbrow – the melting pot   48

Glossary   50

Learn more about Johannesburg   51

Index   52

eGoli – the city of gold

eGoli – the city of gold – is the name given to Johannesburg by the African people of South Africa. This brash, young city owes its existence to the discovery and mining of gold. Less than a hundred years ago, lions and other wild animals roamed the veld where this modern metropolis now stands. Today it is the centre of the world's largest gold-mining industry.

Johannesburg, like many other big cities in the world, faces numerous problems, ranging from crime to pollution. But the biggest and most serious problem is the racial conflict between whites and blacks. The black majority, who have made an immense contribution to the growth of the city through their labour, are treated as second-class citizens. White people from other parts of South Africa are free to come to the city to live and work. This is not the case for the Africans – they have to have permission. Many of them are arrested every day for being in the city 'illegally'.

This problem hangs like a dark and ominous cloud over the city. Some people say there is no problem and that the blacks are happy and content. But, though people might smile and act politely towards one another on the streets, there is a simmering tension just beneath the surface.

The younger generation of black people are angry and bitter. Many of them have lost all faith in securing change through peaceful means and are convinced that they will only win their freedom through armed struggle. All previous peaceful attempts to get the Government to change its policies have failed.

The tragedy of Johannesburg is that the city is rich enough to provide a good life with plenty of opportunities for all its citizens.

Children playing on the boundary dividing white from Coloured areas.

4

The main street of
Johannesburg in 1891.

From mining camp to modern metropolis

Johannesburg – one of the youngest cities in the world – started life as a mining camp. Today, it is the most modern and prosperous city on the African continent, and one of the most important financial centres of the world.

In 1886, prospectors searching for gold in the Transvaal made an exciting discovery on a farm called Randjeslaagte. They unearthed, just below the surface of the barren veld, a rich vein of the precious yellow metal. This was the beginning of one of the biggest gold rushes in history.

People trekked from all over the world to seek their fortunes on the Witwatersrand ('Ridge of White Waters') – a chain of gold-bearing hills. Within months, thousands of prospectors were living in a tented city that later became Johannesburg – the town of Johannes. There were a number of important men connected with the founding of the city whose Christian names were Johannes, but nobody is quite sure which one of them the city is named after.

The first years of the town were feverishly active. The opening of new mines and engineering workshops was an almost daily occurrence. But these were also years of great hardship. Many people were killed by outbreaks of disease as a result of unsanitary conditions and lack of clean water.

For the first five years, food, clothing, machinery and building materials had to be transported to Johannesburg by mules or ox-wagons from distant ports like Cape Town and Durban. The building of the first railway link with Cape Town made a tremendous impact on the growth of the city. Churches, schools, and public buildings took shape. The tents, mud and tin shacks of the mining camps made way for proper brick and concrete houses.

The wealth of the city attracted thousands of people.

Workers make their way to the goldfields during the early days of South African mining.

The absence of ladies in Johannesburg's early days led to the habit of gold-diggers dancing with each other.

A street in Johannesburg at the turn of the century.

Shops, businesses and factories mushroomed virtually overnight. New suburbs had to be built to accommodate the growing population. The city is still growing. Buildings in the central area are continually being pulled down and replaced by tower blocks that dominate the skyline.

School students pour water on a child following a tear gas attack during riots in Soweto.

The racial problem

It is not possible to describe life in Johannesburg without first explaining the racial problem which exists all over South Africa.

There have been clashes between blacks and whites ever since the first Europeans arrived in South Africa more than three hundred years ago. The first settlers were Dutch traders who established a colony at Cape Town in 1652. These people were the forefathers of the white Afrikaner nation. They soon regarded South Africa as their only home and spoke a language, Afrikaans, which derived from Dutch. They were followed much later by British immigrants.

The settlers had little understanding of the language, culture, traditions and religions of the black peoples and considered them inferior. Many of the blacks, including young children, were forced into slavery. Much of their land was taken and heavy taxes imposed on them.

The whites, who are in the minority, have always felt threatened by the blacks. The Afrikaners, in particular, feel they have to protect and preserve their racial identity, culture and religion. South Africa has been ruled by the Afrikaner-dominated Nationalist Party since 1948. Since it took office, this government has passed numerous laws based on their philosophy of apartheid (separation of the races) to protect their way of life. These laws prevent the black majority from having any say in the running of the country.

The Government's policy is that the African people are not citizens of South Africa and can only exercise political rights in the so-called 'Bantu homelands'. These are ten tribal territories carved out of the scattered patches of African reserves that remained after the white conquest of South Africa in the nineteenth century.

The 'homelands' comprise only 14 per cent of the total area of the country. They contain no industrialized areas and are, on the whole, poor and impoverished. Almost half the men in the homelands have to seek work as migrant labourers in 'white' South Africa to support their families.

The Nationalist Party feels that its policy of apartheid is the correct and only way to achieve peace and prosperity in the country. They fear that if the black people were given equal rights with the whites and allowed to vote, then the whites would lose their freedom because they are out-numbered by the blacks.

Critics of the Government argue that the policies of apartheid are the real cause of the racial problem in South Africa. Racial conflict, they say, is likely to continue until all races have full political rights.

Afrikaner settlers trek into the interior of South Africa.

Living with apartheid

South Africa is the only country in the world where racial discrimination is written into the laws of the land. Whites and blacks have to live in separate areas in cities, towns and the countryside. Education and health services are segregated. Blacks have to use separate transport and even ambulances. In almost every case, the services for whites are much better than those for blacks. Africans, Coloureds and Indians, who form more than 80 per cent of the population, have been given only a small percentage of the land. Their share of the country's wealth is less than a quarter.

Rights and freedoms, which are taken for granted by citizens in many countries of the world, are denied to the black people of South Africa: the right to travel freely from one part of the country to another; the right to a decent family life; the right to live where they choose; and the right to elect their own representatives in government.

The Government's policy is that Africans living in the 'white' areas are only there to serve the needs of the white economy – that is, to work in the white-owned factories and mines. They can be resettled at any stage, and thousands have been, in one of the ten tribal homelands, if they are no longer useful to the economy. This applies to many old men and women, or the wives and children of male workers.

The Coloureds and Indians have no 'homelands' and live in segregated areas within 'white' South Africa. More than half a million of these people have been resettled in other areas.

Recently the South African Government has liberalised its policy in some areas. Public amenities, such as recreation facilities and toilets have been desegregated and hotel owners may soon have the choice of admitting blacks.

Left
Black children gaze through a fence that separates them from the white community.

Below
Children play in a park while their nanny looks on.

The heart of commerce and industry

Johannesburg city centre.

Johannesburg is the vital, throbbing heart of the South African economy. A powerhouse of finance, banking and business, it is the centre of a vast industrial region that produces more than 40 per cent of the country's goods and services.

The discovery of gold and the development of a massive mining industry played a major role in the growth of the financial and industrial giant that Johannesburg is today. Shortly after gold was discovered, dozens of foundries, engineering shops and factories were established to supply equipment to the mines. Increasing numbers of people came to the city to seek their fortunes. New industries and commercial enterprises sprang up.

The city lies at the centre of a vast triangular area known as the Pretoria-Witwatersrand-Vereeniging complex. It covers more than 20,000 square kilometres (7,722 square miles). This is the most important industrial, commercial and manufacturing area on the African continent. An enormous range of consumer and industrial goods are manufactured in this region. Many world-famous firms, such as IBM, Olivetti, Esso and AEG Telefunken, have factories there.

Johannesburg is landlocked, but goods are transported to and from the city by an efficient road and railway network. Three airports, including the international Jan Smuts Airport, also provide an important link between the city and other parts of South Africa and the world.

As the country's financial centre, Johannesburg is where most of the capital is raised for South Africa's expansion. One of the most important institutions for this purpose is the Johannesburg Stock Exchange, which was established a

A busy shopping street in Johannesburg city centre.

Pouring liquid gold to make ingots.

year after the discovery of gold. All the major banks and insurance companies have their headquarters in the city.

Johannesburg is the most important shopping centre in the country. People come there from all over the country to buy diamonds, jewellery, clothes, furniture and a wide range of consumer goods. It is also the major centre for important business conferences, exhibitions and shows.

SOWETO

TV
Tower

Zoo

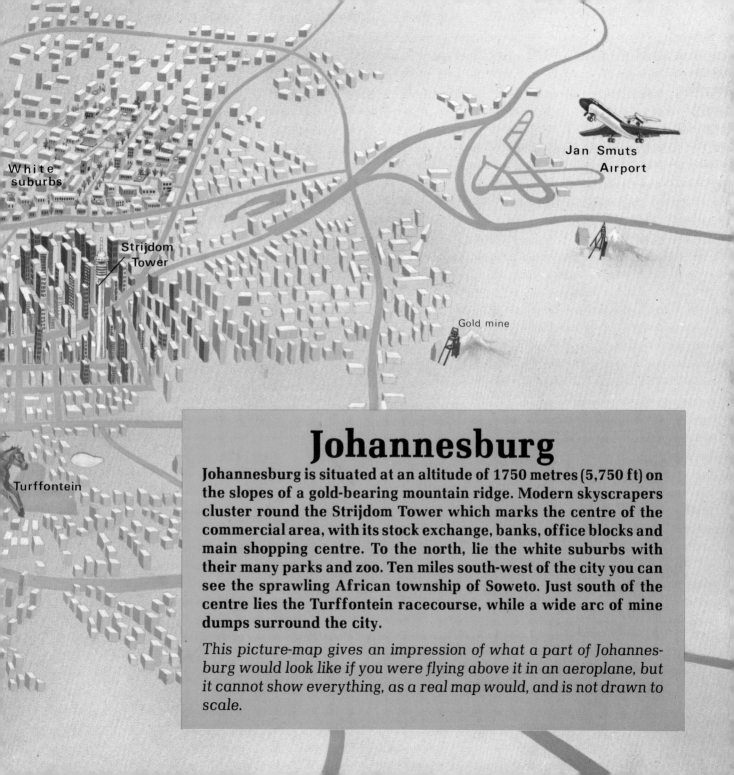

White suburbs

Strijdom Tower

Turffontein

Jan Smuts Airport

Gold mine

Johannesburg

Johannesburg is situated at an altitude of 1750 metres (5,750 ft) on the slopes of a gold-bearing mountain ridge. Modern skyscrapers cluster round the Strijdom Tower which marks the centre of the commercial area, with its stock exchange, banks, office blocks and main shopping centre. To the north, lie the white suburbs with their many parks and zoo. Ten miles south-west of the city you can see the sprawling African township of Soweto. Just south of the centre lies the Turffontein racecourse, while a wide arc of mine dumps surround the city.

This picture-map gives an impression of what a part of Johannesburg would look like if you were flying above it in an aeroplane, but it cannot show everything, as a real map would, and is not drawn to scale.

The gold miners

Day and night, thousands of miners toil deep underground, digging for the gold that has made Johannesburg the wealthiest city in Africa. As one shift returns to the surface, another prepares to descend thousands of metres to find the precious metal.

At the turn of the century, miners worked by candlelight, using hammers, chisels, and hand-drills to extract the gold-bearing ore from the earth. Today's mines are very modern. High-speed skips transport men and equipment deep underground in a matter of minutes. Explosives, powerful drilling equipment, efficient lighting and ventilation have made working conditions easier.

Although mining is much safer now, it is still a dangerous job, requiring courage and immense physical stamina. Some of the mines around Johannesburg are nearly five kilometres deep, and are extremely hot places – the natural temperature of the rock at that depth is 45°C. And then there is the dust and noise, explosions and pneumatic drills. To clear some of the choking dust thrown out by the drills, fine sprays of water are played on to the rock. This means that everyone kneels or lies in pools of water. The most dangerous part of the work is the blasting out of the gold-bearing rock with dynamite. Despite strict safety precautions, accidents do occur, and hundreds of miners have died since gold was first discovered in Johannesburg in 1886. Rock-falls, flooding and mechanical failure have also taken their toll. Mining engineers are continually striving to improve safety and working conditions.

The majority of miners are migrant workers from the rural areas of South Africa. Their wages are low and they live in crowded hostels, where they are not allowed to have their wives and children with them. The main managerial and supervisory posts are occupied by white miners.

Visitors to a gold mine watch a worker finish a new ingot of gold.

Miners drilling underground.

The African townships

Sixteen kilometres (10 miles) south-west of Johannesburg lies the African township of Soweto. This huge town, separated from the city by a large industrial area, is home for more than one million people.

The shortage of accommodation in Soweto is so acute that many people are forced to share. Typical houses in the township consist of four rooms only, and are occupied by between 7 and 14 persons.

Conditions are rather primitive in the large majority of these 'matchbox' houses, as they are called by the residents. Few of them have indoor toilets, a bath or shower, or electricity. Only a quarter of the houses have running cold water inside. Most homes use candles, paraffin or gas lamps for lighting. Coal stoves are used in almost all the homes for heating and cooking and, as a result, Soweto is often shrouded in a haze of greyish-brown smoke, particularly in winter.

In Soweto, and in the township of Alexandra, to the north of the city, are the hostels for migrant workers. Thousands of men and women live in these large, barrack-type buildings. Between four and eight people share a tiny room in these single-sex hostels. There is no heating and all facilities are communal. The migrant workers, many of whom are married with families, cannot receive visitors of the opposite sex in their rooms, even if they are children.

Such social problems as alcoholism and violence are common, and Soweto has the highest murder rate of any city in the world. However, despite the hardships of township life, the African people remain surprisingly good-natured and friendly. They joke and laugh, sing and dance and maintain a lively spirit. Many people make attractive gardens and take good care of their homes.

A child uses a communal water tap in Soweto.

Entertainment facilities are scarce in Soweto. There are a few dance halls and a cinema. Most of the government-owned beer-halls were destroyed during the riots of 1976. *Shebeens* – illegal pubs in private homes – are very popular, although they are frequently raided by the police.

White people are not able to visit the African townships without a permit. Very few of them know much about the townships or the way of life of their inhabitants.

Left
A playground in Soweto.

Below
Living quarters for migrant workers in Soweto.

The Coloured, Indian and Chinese quarters

The Coloureds (people of mixed race) are descended from the first white settlers and the native black peoples. Most Coloureds live in the Cape Province, the most southerly province of South Africa, but many of them have moved to Johannesburg in search of better jobs.

The Indian people of Johannesburg are descended from the labourers that were 'imported' from India by the British, to work on the sugar cane plantations in the province of Natal. When their contracts expired, some of the labourers chose to stay on in South Africa. Some of them became merchants and traders and quite a large number moved to Johannesburg to seek their fortune in the city of gold.

Many Coloureds and Indians were born, and grew up, in the poorer 'white' parts of the city. Despite their poverty, these areas were amongst the most colourful and lively in Johannesburg. They were a favourite haunt of many shoppers in search of exotic goods from the East. The narrow streets were filled with a variety of interesting shops and stalls and the sounds of brisk trading.

Today, many of these areas have been demolished to make way for new 'white' housing and businesses. Thousands of Coloured and Indian families have been forced to resettle in the segregated areas on the outskirts of the city. In these townships there is a severe shortage of houses and overcrowding is common. The Johannesburg City Council is making an attempt to improve the quality of life in these areas by providing better housing and more recreation facilities.

The Chinese, who form a small minority, live mainly in an area of down-town Johannesburg known as 'Chinatown'. For them too, the future is uncertain. A few hundred

An Indian family.

Right
Housing in a coloured township on the outskirts of Johannesburg.

Japanese families live in 'white' areas of the city. But, unlike the Chinese, they are considered to be 'honorary whites'. This is because South Africa has important trade links with Japan.

The white suburbs

The white people of the city live in well laid-out suburbs. Houses range from luxurious mansions equipped with swimming pools, tennis courts and expansive gardens, to modest bungalows. Most of these houses have servants' quarters – normally a small room in the backyard.

For the whites there is no shortage of suitable accommodation, and modern houses are continually being built in new suburbs to house the growing population. Roads are tarred and lined with shady trees, and there is adequate street lighting. There are numerous parks, cinemas, shops, sports and recreation facilities.

Many white families employ a black servant girl to clean

Children play in a paddling pool in a white residential area.

A rather bored looking nanny looks after a white child.

the house, wash the dishes, look after the children and cook the meals. Their gardens are often tended by blacks, who also do various other domestic chores.

The good life in the white suburbs is, however, plagued with fear: there are numerous burglaries. Most families own at least one firearm and houses are protected with burglar-proofing or sophisticated alarm systems. There is also the threatening prospect of a mass uprising by the blacks. Many people fear that one day their domestic servants might turn on them and kill them. As a result, home-owners are investing in radio equipment to enable them to maintain contact with neighbours and police in case of an emergency. More and more whites are forming armed vigilante groups to protect lives and property should the need arise.

A secondary school class at work.

Off to school

In Johannesburg, as in the rest of South Africa, the different racial groups are segregated into different schools. Education is free and compulsory for white children, who start school at the age of five. For Coloured and Indian children, schooling is free but not compulsory, while for African children, education is neither free nor compulsory. If their parents can afford to pay the fees, and buy books and uniforms, African children will start school at the age of seven. However, African parents are so keen to give their children an education that they are prepared to make very big sacrifices to see that their sons and daughters do go to school.

For their first two years, most African children attend schools where a double session, or 'hot seat' system operates – half the children attend lessons in the morning, and the other half in the afternoon. To begin with, they are given instruction in their own tribal language, but after the second year they have to learn all their subjects in English. The curriculum in African schools lays heavy emphasis on manual work, religion, domestic service and 'tribal history'. The schools are overcrowded, and often there are not enough funds available for science equipment, sports facilities and other teaching aids. In 1976 the authorities tried to introduce a new practice whereby African children would have to be taught in both English and Afrikaans. This was one of the causes of the Soweto riots, in which many black children were killed during clashes with the police.

At least half of African children drop out, for financial reasons, by the end of their fourth year at school. Following the troubles of 1976, the South African Government promised to introduce free education for all races, and some plans to implement this have been drawn up.

Primary school children concentrate hard on their writing.

Finding a job

Queues begin forming outside the African labour bureau shortly after sunrise. Those people who are desperate to find a job, know that it is vital to get there early. But even a good place in the queue is no guarantee of work, for unemployment is rising and the competition for jobs is intense. South Africa has no Social Security system and for those without a job the future is bleak and insecure. They face eviction from their accommodation and, in many cases, expulsion to rural areas.

Every African seeking work has to register at a labour bureau before he can take on a job. To register, he must have his reference book – an identity document which Africans over the age of 16 must carry with them at all times. The information in this 'stinker', as it is called by Africans, dictates where they may live and work. Only those Africans who have work are entitled to live in Johannesburg. Those who cannot find a job risk being sent away to the distant tribal reserves. In spite of this law, thousands of Africans continue to live 'illegally' in the city in the hope that they will eventually find a job.

The majority of jobs available to Africans are unskilled and low paid. Even those few who have succeeded in obtaining a good education are often unable to find skilled, well-paid jobs. These are reserved for whites – thousands of whom are immigrants from Europe. Most blacks become domestic servants, gardeners, miners, labourers, messengers, drivers or factory workers. A life of crime is often the alternative for the jobless.

Finding a job is much simpler for the white worker. A wide range of positions are available, and wages are very much higher than those of black workers. White trade unions are allowed to negotiate on behalf of their members, but black workers' trade unions are not officially recognized.

26

Right
Jobless in Johannesburg.

Below
Africans brandish their hated passes before burning them during demonstrations in 1960.

On the streets

More than a thousand young black children live on the streets of the city. They survive on what they can beg or steal and often die from starvation, exposure or the effects of glue-sniffing. Sniffing glue relieves the feeling of hunger and makes them feel drunk.

Selling newspapers is one way that homeless children can earn a bit of money.

These urchins – some of them only six years old – come from homes where the families are too poor to support them. Others are orphans, or the victims of broken homes. They sleep in alleyways, shop doorways, disused warehouses or in rough temporary shelters on waste ground.

They beg at bus stops, and outside cinemas and restaurants, for money to buy a loaf of bread and some milk – their main diet. Some of them earn a bit of money by selling newspapers, shining shoes, running errands or acting as 'unofficial' parking attendants. Many fall into a life of crime – shoplifting, snatching handbags or thieving from cars. Others are employed by *tsotsis* (gangsters) as lookouts or decoys. Some have become hardened criminals by the time they reach their early teens.

For these children the city is a jungle where only the strong survive. Those who are sickly or weak fall prey to disease. They risk death through exposure, flu or pneumonia in the winter. Many of them are arrested by the police for vagrancy or theft. In court, they are normally sentenced to a flogging and then they are back on the streets again.

Welfare and church bodies are concerned about these children. Some organizations try to arrange for them to be sent to orphanages or foster homes. But there are a limited number of vacancies, and for many of them the streets will continue to be home.

*A homeless child sleeps
by a hot air vent.*

Family life

The black people of Johannesburg, like people all over the world, cherish the stability and warmth of family life. But, for many of them, the right to live a decent family life is denied by the laws of apartheid. Thousands of families have been split up by these laws.

Black mothers, employed as servants or nannies by white families, are not allowed to have their husbands or children living with them in their backyard rooms. Many fathers have to leave their families behind in the rural areas when they come to the city to work. Those families who are permitted to live together in Johannesburg face problems of overcrowding and low wages. In most black families, the father is very much the head of the household, although it is quite usual for both parents to go out to work. A typical Soweto family might start their day with breakfast at five-thirty a.m. By six o'clock the parents would have to leave the house to join other workers waiting to catch buses and trains into the centre of Johannesburg. Children often have to spend the day with relatives or friends. Many of them are left alone. Younger sisters or brothers have to look after the babies. The children clean up, wash the dishes, do the shopping and make up the fire. The family are not usually together again until the parents return from work between six and seven o'clock in the evening.

In spite of their problems, the black people are fortunate in that their culture is based on the concept of the 'extended' family. Before the blacks moved to the cities, their tribes were, in a sense, an 'extended' version of their own families. This idea of belonging to a larger 'family' is still an important part of black culture. In the black community, many people refer to those of their own age as 'brothers and sisters' or to older people as 'mother and father', even if there is no direct family connection.

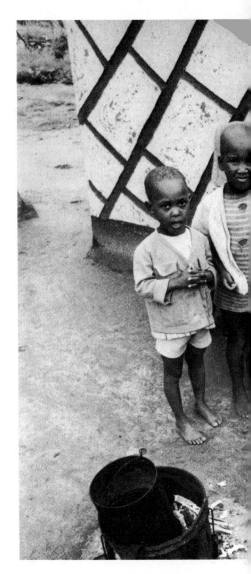

Mother and children are left in the country while the father works 700 kilometres away in Johannesburg.

Right

A woman attends to the tear in her grandson's shorts.

31

What people eat

Most black people live on a staple diet of maize-meal porridge (*putu*) which is eaten for breakfast, lunch and dinner. If the family can afford it, they will have milk with the *putu* at breakfast, and bread with butter. In the evening the *putu* is eaten with vegetables and spiced with curry powder. Meat is normally a luxury reserved for Sundays or special occasions. *Putu* is made by slowly heating the maize-meal flour with a bit of water in a large pot. It forms into thick lumps which are often eaten by hand.

Fish and chip shops in the city do a brisk trade, particularly at lunchtime and after work. They also sell such items as meatballs, curried eggs and chicken pieces. Some of them also sell *putu*. There are very few restaurants in Johannesburg that sell traditional African food, but those that do are well patronized.

In the black community, everybody looks forward to big

White South Africans love a barbecue.

Below
Infants suffering from malnutrition in a black hospital in Johannesburg.

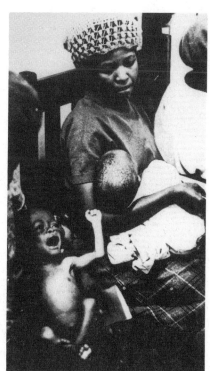

occasions like weddings or funerals, when the hosts traditionally lay on a feast. At very special occasions – or if the hosts can afford it – a whole ox will be roasted over a fire. Even at feasts, *putu* is the main course. There is also a good selection of vegetables, puddings and cakes prepared in the Western style.

But, feasts are rare, and for many thousands of black people in the city, hunger is a grim reality. Many black children, especially those under two years old, suffer from the effects of malnutrition. Some of them die.

White South Africans love a *braaivleis* (barbecue). The climate is ideally suited to eating out of doors and many families have a *braaivleis* at least once a month. *Boerewors* (a type of sausage), chops and steak are grilled over an open fire and served with potatoes, corn on the cob, fresh vegetables and *putu* which the whites call *pap*.

The Indians prepare their own traditional dishes and curries. There are a number of Indian and Chinese restaurants in the city which are well patronized by white people with a taste for exotic food.

33

A day in the park

At the weekend and on public holidays the people of Johannesburg flock to the parks. Acres of rolling green grass, banks of beautiful flowers, shady trees, lakes and ponds provide a welcome sanctuary from the bustle and noise of the city. There are more than 600 parks in and around the city. Some are no bigger than a few acres. Others are vast, and include sports and entertainment facilities.

For the black workers and their families, a day in a park is an opportunity to relax and have fun. The majority of the parks are situated in the white suburbs and this means train and bus fares. But it is well worth it. The children can enjoy a ride on the swings or play a game of soccer. Or the whole family can go rowing on a lake.

Most families take their own picnic lunches because the restaurants in the parks are only open to whites. This also applies to swimming pools and tennis courts. Black parents find it difficult to explain to their children why they are only allowed to do some of the things the white children do. It is only recently, for example, that blacks have been allowed to sit on park benches in Johannesburg.

One of the most exciting outings is a trip to the zoo. Here, in the largest park in Johannesburg, thousands of animals, birds and reptiles are on display. Most of the animals are African, but, there is also the opportunity to see species from remote parts of the world, such as polar bears. There is also a children's section, where youngsters can play with farm and domestic animals.

Parks in the city are very popular with workers and flat dwellers. They can eat their lunches on well-tended lawns and share a few crumbs with the pigeons and sparrows. These parks also provide space for an impromptu ball game, or a heated game of cards or dominoes.

Trade exhibitions are sometimes held in Johannesburg's parks.

Schoolchildren on a
day's outing at the zoo.

Music and dancing

The modern metropolis of Johannesburg pulsates with rhythm. Intermingled with the hum and roar of the city are the sounds of many different types of music – everything from the ancient beat of Africa to modern jazz and pop.

Music and dancing have always been an integral part of the culture of the African people – a means of expressing the joy and sadness of life, telling stories or simply having fun. Contact with the whites has had a strong effect on their music. Today it is a fusion of vibrant African rhythms, jazz, rock and roll and a variety of other influences.

Impromptu musical performances are common on the streets of the city. Solitary musicians or small groups of players set up their equipment where they will be assured of a good audience. Music fills the streets and people dance, clap or sing. Sometimes, a group of mineworkers travelling through the city from one of the rural areas, will set up their drums on a pavement and perform an exhilarating tribal dance. Young men play their guitars as they walk through the streets, and portable radios, with their volumes at full blast, are a common feature.

The townships, too, are alive with music. Most houses have a radio or record player and toddlers learn to dance virtually before they walk. Dancing at clubs and discos is a favourite activity.

The white people also enjoy music and dancing. Youngsters, like their contemporaries in Europe and America, buy all the latest records and enjoy learning new dance steps from abroad.

This young boy seems to be enjoying his piano lesson.

African dancers in Johannesburg.

A wealth of religions

Children wear their best clothes to attend a church service.

Johannesburg is a city rich in religion. The many different race and language groups from all over the world, who have made Johannesburg their home, brought their religions with them. Christian churches of every denomination, Jewish synagogues, Muslim mosques and Hindu temples are scattered in and around the city.

The majority of the blacks are Christians, belonging to a variety of sects – Roman Catholic, Anglican, Lutheran, Presbyterian, Methodist and Apostolic. The Independent Church has the largest following, but very few churches. Members, identified by their blue and white robes, gather and hold services wherever a few of them get together. Street corners, backyards, waste grounds – all can serve as a suitable site.

The Church's doctrine is a blend of Christianity and traditional African tribal religion. Much of the service is devoted to singing, dancing, going into trances and communicating with the spirits of dead ancestors.

For many people, going to church is something of a special social occasion. It is not only a religious activity, but an opportunity to meet with friends, joke, dance, and sing.

Witchdoctors still play an important part in black religious life and there are more than a thousand in Johannesburg. *Sangomas* (female witchdoctors) and *Inyangas* (male witchdoctors) are often consulted by people in trouble. The witchdoctors are called upon to cast out evil spirits and cure ailments ranging from mental illness to toothache, with the help of magic phrases and herbalism.

Most Afrikaners belong to the Dutch Reformed Church which wields considerable influence in the political affairs of the country. The English-speaking population are mainly Anglicans, Roman Catholics, Methodists or Presbyterians.

There are a number of Jewish synagogues, a sprinkling of Greek Orthodox churches and even a small Russian Orthodox church. Richly-decorated Hindu temples and beautiful mosques serve the religious needs of Johannesburg's Asian community.

Children play in the dirt roads outside their local church.

The thrill of sport

Coloured children make their own sport with the help of a rubber tyre.

The people of Johannesburg love sport. The mild, exhilarating climate is suitable for a wide range of summer and winter sports. There are excellent facilities for almost every conceivable type of activity, from athletics to water polo. Many of these amenities, however, are reserved for whites only.

Soccer is the most popular sport amongst blacks. On the dusty streets and vacant lots of the black townships, there is always a game of soccer in progress. A real leather soccer ball or a good pair of boots are cherished possessions to any black youngster. Most aspiring young soccer stars practise barefoot with anything from a tennis ball to a bundle of tightly bound rags. Many of them dream that one day they will play in proper kit for one of the top teams.

There are numerous soccer clubs and leagues in the black townships. Nearly everybody is a keen fan of one of the top rival clubs. The excitement at big matches is intense, as thousands of supporters turn out to cheer the players.

The long, hot summer makes swimming a very popular sport. Many whites have their own private swimming pools, or swim in one of the public pools in the suburbs. The blacks have fewer swimming pools and as a result they are very crowded.

Rugby is the most popular sport amongst whites, particularly the Afrikaners. At most schools it is compulsory for the boys to play rugby. Major rugby matches are very important occasions in the white community. Members of the Government, including the Prime Minister, attend and tickets change hands for astronomical sums of money.

The one thing many Johannesburg sport fans miss is the thrill of seeing their sportsmen and women compete in international events. South Africa has been banned from most international sporting associations and sports events,

One of South Africa's first 'mixed race' rugby clubs in action.

including the Olympic Games. This has happened because the Government's apartheid policy does not allow equal opportunity for sportsmen of different races to represent their country.

Getting around

Johannesburg has an efficient network of roads and motor-ways, linking the city with the surrounding suburbs, and giving swift access for those possessing a car. Public transport is segregated on racial lines. Coloureds and Indians have recently been allowed to travel on the same buses as whites, while a separate service exists for the Africans. Their green single-decker buses are disparagingly referred to as 'green mambas' (a deadly snake) because of the number of accidents they are involved in. These are usually caused by overloading or poor maintenance.

But the majority of African workers travel by train. There are about 500 trains running in and out of Soweto and Johannesburg daily, carrying almost half a million people in both directions. These trains are packed to capacity. Seating is limited and most passengers have to stand.

There are many dangers involved in catching these trains, but there is little option, since it is the cheapest form of transport. There have been a number of serious train accidents on the Soweto–Johannesburg line, involving hundreds of deaths and thousands of injuries. This is because of the unsafe conditions caused by overcrowding, strain and the often reckless way that they are driven.

The trains are notorious for the limited amount of time they allow for passengers to get on or off and there is always a mad scramble at stations. Handbags, parcels, shoes and hats are often lost as the rushing crowd surges on and off. Young daredevils called 'staff riders' often jump on to moving trains and cling to precarious footholds to get a free ride.

Inside the trains there is a danger from the 'tsotsi' (gangster) element, who pick pockets or attack their victims with knives or sharpened bicycle spokes and rob them of pay packets or parcels.

African workers struggle onto a grossly over-crowded train.

Below
Railway terminal at Queen Elizabeth Bridge, Johannesburg.

Press, television and radio

Johannesburg is the centre of South Africa's media industry. All the major daily and Sunday newspapers are printed there, and it is also the headquarters of the government-controlled South African Broadcasting Corporation. Seven dailies, three Sunday newspapers and a variety of monthly and weekly periodicals are published in the city.

Newspapers are severely restricted in what they may report, and journalists and editors face heavy jail sentences, or fines, for disclosing certain information. In some cases, the Government can close a newspaper down if it feels it is stepping out of line. As a result, matters relating to prisons, the police, atomic energy or anything to do with the security of the state are treated with caution by journalists.

The English-language Press, which includes black newspapers, have protested vigorously at the erosion of their freedom by the Government. They demand the right to keep their readers informed of developments in all spheres of life. But with so many laws, it is a difficult job. In spite of this they continue to report on, and criticize many aspects of Government policy which they consider unjust and oppressive. They carry stories which the Afrikaans newspapers or Government-controlled broadcasting media omit to report.

Television is a very new phenomenon in South Africa. For many years the Government blocked the introduction of TV on the grounds that it would 'destroy the morals of the nation'. Five years ago, however, the 'little box' made its appearance. Programmes alternate between English and Afrikaans, and open and close with religious programmes. As yet there is no TV service for blacks, although one is planned. The radio section of the SABC broadcasts on 20 different stations in 23 languages to all parts of South Africa and abroad.

The new television centre of the South African Broadcasting Corporation.

44

Urban protest

The violent clatter of automatic gunfire, devastating explosions from rockets, bombs and hand grenades and the shrill sirens of emergency vehicles, are becoming an increasing feature of life in Johannesburg.

Acts of 'urban terrorism' have risen dramatically in the last four years. Most white families own at least one gun. Houses, businesses and public facilities are heavily protected by security alarms. More important installations are guarded by armed men and dogs. All white, and a few black, policemen are armed. Special army units can be called within minutes to deal with an outbreak of violence.

For years the demands of the black people of South Africa for changes have been ignored by the Government. Leaders and members of organizations calling for peaceful change have been imprisoned, banned and even assassinated. Resistance movements, such as the African National Congress of South Africa, eventually decided that their demands would never be met by peaceful means, and some members embarked on a programme of guerrilla warfare. Police stations, telephone exchanges and vital rail and fuel installations have all come under attack.

The 'terrorists' as they are called by the whites, or 'freedom fighters' as they are known by the blacks, feel that the circumstances of South Africa make it necessary to fight. They receive training in guerrilla warfare in neighbouring African states and certain overseas countries. Many of them fled after the protests in Soweto in June 1976, when many people were killed and wounded. It is a tragedy for Johannesburg and South Africa that a situation has been reached where violence is used.

Children hand out African National Congress leaflets — or try to!

A child has been shot dead in the Soweto riots of 1976.

Hillbrow – the 'melting pot'

Hillbrow – the most densely populated area of Johannesburg – is the cosmopolitan 'melting pot' of the city. Here, in blocks of high-rise flats, live thousands of people. Many of them are immigrants from different parts of the world. More and more black people, particularly Coloureds and Indians, are illegally moving into 'flatland' because of the severe housing shortage in their own areas. Officially it is a 'white' area but it is fast becoming multiracial.

This is the most lively part of the city, boasting numerous nightclubs, discos, restaurants and cinemas. Many young people are drawn to Hillbrow because of its lively international atmosphere. Record bars and boutiques, stocked with the latest fashions, are all part of the attraction. Some of the restaurants and nightspots have been permitted to admit blacks. In many ways, Hillbrow leads the city in the field of good race relations. Blacks and whites are learning to live together and so set an example for the rest of the country.

Hillbrow has a high crime rate. The sounds of gunshots and screams are frequently heard at night. There are regular

A fashionable shop in Hillbrow.

Taking a break in a cafe in the Hillbrow district.

arrests for drunkenness, illegal gambling and drug dealing.

It has, despite the violence, an irresistible appeal for the people of Johannesburg. Many shops stay open until late at night, and one big food store is open day and night throughout the year. The streets are crowded with people and there are restaurants offering food from Chinese beansprouts to German frankfurters. On New Year's Eve, thousands of people make their way to Hillbrow to sing and dance in the streets until the early hours. Good-natured chaos reigns and even the police join in the merrymaking.

49

Glossary

Afrikaans	The language of the Afrikaner people. English and Afrikaans are the two official languages of South Africa.
Afrikaners	Descendants of the original Dutch and French settlers who came to South Africa in the seventeenth century. Today, they are the ruling minority in the country.
Apartheid	The Afrikaans name for the Government's policy of racial segregation.
Blacks	The African people of the country. It is also used as a collective term for the African, Coloured and Indian people.
Coloureds	People of mixed race resulting from intermarriage of whites and blacks.
Homelands	There are ten tribal homelands in South Africa for the different African ethnic groups.
Malnutrition	A condition arising from a lack of nourishing food. The symptoms include outbreaks of sores, swollen stomachs, apathy and listlessness.
Migrant labourers	Men and women who leave their families behind in the rural areas to work in the city.
Putu	Maize-meal porridge, the staple diet of the Africans.
Soweto	The vast African township south-west of Johannesburg.
Transvaal	The most northerly of South Africa's four provinces and the richest in gold. Johannesburg is situated in the southern part of this province.
Tsotsis	The notorious gangsters and criminals of the African townships.
Urban terrorism	Acts of violence, including sabotage, to achieve political aims.
Veld	South African name for a grassy landscape with very few trees.
Whites	The term used to refer to all people of European origin.

Learn more about Johannesburg

Books for younger readers
> *Let's visit South Africa* by Bernard Newman. (Burke Books)
> *Southern Africa* by R. Clayton. (Hart-Davis Educational)
> *This is Apartheid.* A short pamphlet illustrated with 50 pictures available from IDAF publications, 104 Newgate Street, London EC1A 7AP.
> *We Live in South Africa* by Jack Viviers.

Books for older readers
> *A window on Soweto* by Joyce Sikakane
> *Whirlwind before the storm.* Alan Brooks and Jeremy Brookhill. A study of the origins and development of the uprising in Soweto and the rest of South Africa from June to December 1976.
> *Forbidden pastures: Education under apartheid* by Freda Troup.
> These books are all available from the same address as the pamphlet 'This is Apartheid'.

Other information sources
> The Information Section, South African Embassy, Trafalgar Square, London WC2N 5 DP
> The Public Relations Office, Johannesburg City Council, Civic Centre, Braamfontein, Johannesburg, South Africa
> Anti-Apartheid Movement, 89 Charlotte Street, London W1PD 2 DQ
> The African National Congress of South Africa, P.O. Box 38, 28 Penton Street, London N1 9PR

Picture acknowledgements

Camera Press 26, 33 (above), 36, 43; International Defence and Aid Fund for Southern Africa 4, 8, 10–11 (below), 18, 20–21, 22, 23, 24, 25, 28, 29, 30, 31, 33 (below), 37, 40, 46, 47; Mansell 5, 7 (below), 9; South African Broadcasting Company 45; South African Embassy frontispiece 12, 13 (both), 17, 19 (above), 21, 34, 35, 41, 48, 49; South African Tourist Board 32, 42; United Nations 10–11 (above), 16–17, 19 (below); United Society for the Propogation of the Gospel 27, 38, 39; Wayland Picture Library 6, 7 (above).
The cover picture is by Spectrum.
The coloured map appearing on pages 14–15 is by Bill Donohoe.

Index

Afrikaans 8, 25
African National Congress 46
Apartheid 8, 9, 10, 30, 41

Bantu Homelands 8, 10, 26
British 8
Buses 42

Capetown 6, 8
Cape Province 20
Censorship 44
Christians 38
Churches 6, 28, 38
Coloureds 10, 20, 25, 42, 48
Commerce 12
Crime 26, 28

Dancing 37
Durban 6

Education 25
Entertainment 19, 22

Factories 7
Feasts 33
Finance 12
Food 32

Gangsters 28, 42
Goldmining 4, 6, 12, 16–17

Health Services 10

Hillbrow 48
Hindus 38
Homeless children 28
Housing 18, 20, 22, 48

Identity documents 26
Industry 12

Jan Smuts Airport 12
Johannesburg City Council 20

Map of Johannesburg 14–15
Migrant workers 16, 18
Music 37
Muslims 38

Natal 20
Nationalist Party 8, 9
Newspapers 44
Nightclubs 48

Parks 34
Police 4, 25, 28, 44, 46, 49
Putu 32

Race relations 4, 8, 9, 10, 19, 20,
    23, 25, 46, 48
Races of Johannesburg
    Afrikaners 8, 38, 40, 44
    Chinese 20, 33
    Coloureds 10, 20, 25, 42, 48
    Dutch 8

English 25, 38, 44
Indians 10, 20, 25, 33, 42, 48
Japanese 20
Religion 38
Restaurants 32, 49
Rugby 40

SABC 44
Schools 6, 25
Servants 22, 26
Shopping 13, 49
Soccer 40
Social Security 26
South African Government 8, 9,
    10, 25, 40, 44, 46
Soweto 18–19, 30, 42
    riots 25, 46
Sports 40–41
Staff riders 42

Television 44
Terrorism 46
Trade Union 26
Trains 42
Transvaal 6

White suburbs 22
Witchdoctors 38
Witwatersrand 6
Work 26

Zoo 34